Gallup Guides for Youth Facing Persistent Prejudice

People with Mental and Physical Challenges

Gallup Guides for Youth Facing Persistent Prejudice

- Asians
- Blacks
- Hispanics
- Jews
- The LGBT Community
- Muslims
- Native North American Indians
- People with Mental and Physical Challenges

GALLUP GUIDES FOR YOUTH FACING PERSISTENT PREJUDICE

People with Mental and Physical Challenges

Ellyn Sanna

Mason Crest

Mason Crest
370 Reed Road
Broomall, Pennsylvania 19008
www.masoncrest.com

Printed and bound in the United States of America.

First printing
9 8 7 6 5 4 3 2 1

ISBN-13: 978-1-4222-2462-5 (hardcover series)
ISBN-13: 978-1-4222-2470-0 (hardcover)
ISBN-13: 978-1-4222-9343-0 (e-book)
ISBN-13: 978-1-4222-2479-3 (paperback)

Library of Congress Cataloging-in-Publication Data

Sanna, Ellyn, 1957-
 Gallup guides for youth facing persistent prejudice. People with mental and physical challenges / by Ellyn Sanna.
     p. cm.
  title: People with mental and physical challenges
 Includes bibliographical references and index.
  ISBN 978-1-4222-2470-0 (hbk.) -- ISBN 978-1-4222-2462-5 (series hbk.) -- ISBN 978-1-4222-2479-3 (pbk.) -- ISBN 978-1-4222-9343-0 (ebook)
 1. Discrimination against people with disabilities--United States--Juvenile literature. 2. Youth with disabilities--United States--Juvenile literature. 3. Youth with mental disabilities--United States--Juvenile literature. 4. People with disabilities--Civil rights--United States--Juvenile literature. 5. People with mental disabilities--Civil rights--United States--Juvenile literature. I. Title. II. Title: People with mental and physical challenges.
 HV1553.S244 2013
 305.9'083--dc23
                        2012017110

Produced by Harding House Publishing Services, Inc.
www.hardinghousepages.com
Interior design by Micaela Sanna.
Page design elements by Cienpies Design / Illustrations | Dreamstime.com.
Cover design by Torque Advertising + Design.

CONTENTS

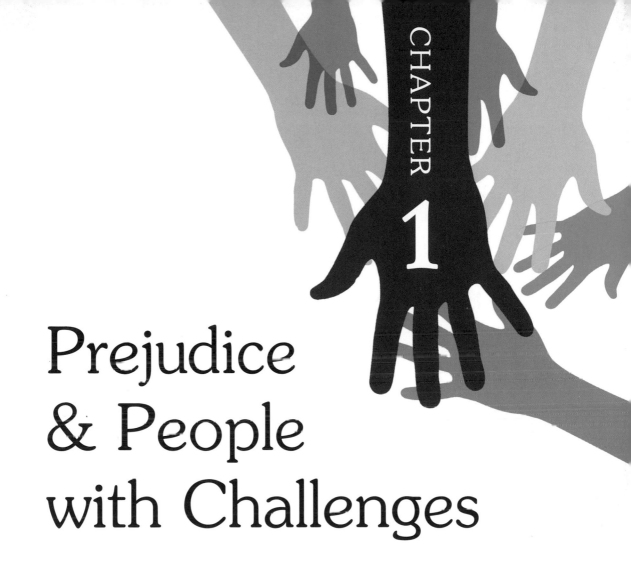

Prejudice & People with Challenges

Imagine sitting in a classroom with thirty-four other students. Look around you. You'll see different outward appearances, clothing styles, personalities, and interests. But what may or may not be visible are the challenges each person in the classroom faces.

What Is a Disability?

People use words in different ways. A teacher who is talking about a student with a disability in his classroom may mean something different from what a doctor does when she describes treating someone with a disability. A psychologist may mean something else altogether. So might a lawyer. The World Health Organization (WHO), part of the United Nations (UN), makes these distinctions between impairment, disability, and handicap:

(a) Impairment is "any loss or abnormality of psychological, physiological, or anatomical structure or function." Impairments are disturbances at the level of the organ which include defects in or loss of a limb, organ or other body structure, as well as defects in or loss of a mental function. Examples of impairments include blindness, deafness, loss of sight in an eye, paralysis of a limb, amputation of a limb; mental retardation, partial sight, loss of speech, mutism.

(b) Disability is a "restriction or lack (resulting from an impairment) of ability to perform an activity in the manner or within the range considered normal for a human being." It describes a functional limitation or activity restriction caused by an impairment. Disabilities are descriptions of disturbances in function at the level of the person. Examples of disabilities include difficulty seeing, speaking or hearing; difficulty moving or climbing stairs; difficulty grasping, reaching, bathing, eating, toileting.

(c) A handicap is a "disadvantage for a given individual, resulting from an impairment or disability, that limits or prevents the fulfillment of a role that is normal (depending on age, sex and social and cultural factors) for that individual." The term is also a classification of "circumstances in which disabled people are likely to find themselves." Handicap describes the social and economic roles of impaired or disabled persons that place them at a disadvantage compared to other persons. These disadvantages are brought about through the interaction of the person with specific environments and cultures. Examples of handicaps include being bedridden or confined to home; being unable to use public transport; being socially isolated.

Researchers tell us that in your imaginary class of thirty-four kids, odds are good that:

- five (four boys and one girl) struggle to overcome learning disabilities.
- three have asthma or other respiratory conditions.
- one has a chronic heart condition or is in poor health.
- between four and seven have psychiatric disorders.
- two have disabilities or health problems severe enough to limit their physical activity.
- four require at least part-time special education.

Canada's Disabilities

According to the 2001 census, the disabilities in Canada break down like this:

- mobility 72%
- pain 70%
- agility 67%
- hearing 30%
- sight 17%
- psychological 15%
- learning 13%
- memory 12%
- speech 11%
- developmental 4%
- unknown 3%

Children with disabilities face many challenges in school. Special education classes are designed to help them learn despite these challenges.

According to the U.S. Department of Education, one out of five Americans has a some form of disability. Almost half of these are considered to have a severe disability. In the 2001 census, Statistics Canada found that more than 3.6 million Canadians—12.4 percent of the population, or more than one out of every ten people—had some form of disability. The U.S. Centers for Disease Control and Prevention (CDC) found that at the end of the twentieth century, 68 million Americans were disabled enough to have activity limitations, 61 million of which resulted from chronic health conditions.

The same CDC study reported that 8 million Americans used assistive technology devices (ATDs) to help them move or walk. Another five million used ATDs to help them see or hear. And since then, the numbers have climbed still higher.

Physical disabilities, learning disabilities, psychological disorders—all these issues require support and intervention for the people who face them. People who face physical and mental challenges are a very diverse group. It's impossible to list every sort of disability out there. There are some people with mental challenges, like **obsessive compulsive disorder (OCD)**, **bipolar disorder**, **autism**, or **schizophrenia**. Then there are people with physical challenges, such as **quadriplegia**, blindness, deafness, or brain injuries. Some people with disabilities were born with them. Others became disabled because of a disease or an accident.

Some disabled students need to learn in a separate environment and some can function well in a mainstream classroom. Some people with disabilities use tools to help them get around, and some don't. People with mental and physical challenges are varied group of people! It's impossible to say that they are all one way or another. In fact, current estimates say that there are 650 million people worldwide with some form of disability.

Mental and Physical Challenges

Disability is a common human condition. It should not separate humans from other humans! But it does. Prejudice against people facing physical and mental challenges is all too common.

In 1993, the United Nations (UN) issued this statement: "The place of disabled persons is everywhere. Persons with disabilities should be guaranteed equal opportunity through the elimination of all socially determined barriers, be they

These girls have Down syndrome, a form of mental disability with which they were born.

physical, financial, social or psychological, which exclude or restrict full participation in society." This is the goal that countries around the world are working to meet.

Prejudice is what gets in the way.

WHAT IS PREJUDICE?

The root word of prejudice is "pre-judge." Prejudiced people often judge others based purely on one thing: their race or ethnicity, their religion, their gender, or their abilities. They make assumptions about others that may have no basis in reality. They believe that if you have a mental or physical challenge or your skin is darker or you speak a different language or worship God in a different way, then they already know you are not as smart, not as nice, not as honest, not as valuable, or not as moral as they are. People with mental and physical challenges have long been the victims of prejudice in North America, Europe, and around the world.

Why do human beings experience prejudice? **Sociologists** believe humans have a basic tendency to fear anything that's unfamiliar or unknown. Someone who is strange (in that they're not like us) is scary; they're automatically dangerous or inferior. If we get to know the strangers, of course, we end up discovering that they're not so different from ourselves.

Prejudice Starts Inside

Sociologists have found that people who are prejudiced toward one group of people also tend to be prejudiced toward other groups. In a study done in 1946, people were asked about their attitudes concerning a variety of ethnic groups, including Danireans, Pirraneans, and Wallonians. The study found that people who were prejudiced toward blacks and Jews also distrusted these other three groups. The catch is that Danireans, Pirraneans, and Wallonians didn't exist! This suggests that prejudice's existence may be rooted within the person who feels prejudice rather than in the group that is feared and hated.

They're not so frightening and threatening after all. But too often, we don't let that happen. We put up a wall between the strangers and ourselves. We're on the inside; they're on the outside. And then we peer over the wall, too far away from the people on the other side to see anything but our differences.

And here's where another human tendency comes into play: stereotyping.

Prejudice & People with Challenges

STEREOTYPES

A stereotype is a fixed, commonly held idea or image of a person or group that's based on an **oversimplification** of some observed or imagined trait. Stereotypes assume that whatever is believed about a group is typical for each and every individual within that group. "All blondes are dumb," is a stereotype. "Women are poor drivers," is another. "Men are slobs," is yet another, and "Gay men are **effeminate**," is one as well.

Many stereotypes tend to make us feel superior in some way to the person or group being stereotyped. Not all stereotypes are negative, however; some are positive—"Black men are

High School Stereotypes

The average high school has its share of stereotypes—lumping a certain kind of person together, ignoring all the ways that each person is unique. These stereotypes are often expressed with a single word or phrase: "jock," "nerd," "goth," "prep," or "geek." The images these words call to mind are easily recognized and understood by others. But that doesn't mean they're true!

Group Pressure

Why do people continue to believe stereotypes despite evidence that may not support them? Researchers have found that it may have something to do with group pressure. During one experiment, seven members of a group were asked to state that a short line is longer than a long line. About a third of the rest of the group agreed that the short line was longer, despite evidence to the contrary. Apparently, people conform to the beliefs of those around them in order to gain group acceptance.

good at basketball," "Gay guys have good fashion sense," or "Asian students are smart"—but that doesn't make them true. They ignore individuals' uniqueness. They make assumptions that may or may not be accurate.

We can't help our human tendency to put people into categories. As babies, we faced a confusing world filled with an amazing variety of new things. We needed a way to make sense of it all, so one of our first steps in learning about the world around us was to sort things into separate slots in our heads: small furry things that said *meow* were kitties, while larger furry things that said *arf-arf* were doggies; cars went *vroom-vroom*, but trains were longer and went *choo-choo*; little girls looked one way and little boys another; and doctors wore white coats, while police officers wore blue. These were

Nguyen Thuy Thi (gold medallist) of Vietnam

Mental and Physical Challenges

Disablism

In the United Kingdom, people use the term "disablism." It means extreme prejudice against people with mental and physical challenges. It's like racism or sexism. In the United States, people sometimes use the term "ableism" to mean the same thing. Neither term has really reached the mainstream, though, and many people have never heard them.

our earliest stereotypes. They were a handy way to make sense of the world; they helped us know what to expect, so that each time we faced a new person or thing, we weren't starting all over again from scratch.

But stereotypes become dangerous when we continue to hold onto our mental images despite new evidence. (For instance, as a child you may have decided that all dogs bite—which means that when faced by friendly, harmless dogs, you assume they're dangerous and so you miss out on getting to know all dogs.) Stereotypes are particularly dangerous and destructive when they're directed at persons or groups of persons. That's when they turn into prejudice.

What Should People with Disabilities Expect?

The World Institute on Disability lists the values that they use to promote the rights of people with mental and physical challenges. WID aspires to work in a world with cultures where:

- Disability is a natural part of the human condition.
- People with disabilities have equal rights to their own self-determination.
- People with disabilities drive public policy issues and priorities.
- People with disabilities have the right to make informed choices.
- Information and education promote employment for all.
- People with disabilities have the right to earn a living and live independently.
- Accessible, affordable health care and community supports are essential rights that support employment and well being.
- The disability experience is in the arts, media, and wider culture.

Over time, people with mental and physical challenges have been subject to a number of different stereotypes. In the past, people with disabilities were often considered freaks. They were put on display to be stared at. They were thought to be too inhuman to be able to function in society. Nowadays, most of us know better—but that doesn't mean that new stereotypes about disabilities haven't risen to take the old ones' place. Now, all people with disabilities are often considered to be victims, and to be weak and fragile. Some are thought of as funny and sweet. We see them as objects of laughter or pity, rather than as people we like to get to know.

In reality, people with disabilities are very diverse. In fact, many don't even like the term "disabled" because it implies that they aren't able to do things that "normal" people can do, and that there is a problem with them. People face all sorts of different physical and mental challenges. And they each have a unique personality, a unique history, and a unique story to tell.

CHAPTER 2

History Lesson

Mental and physical challenges are a normal part of human life. Not everyone has a disability, but those who do are not out of the ordinary. For as long as there have been human beings, there have been some individuals who function a little differently. At the same time, people with mental and physical challenges have frequently been treated as different. Sometimes during history, they have been barely tolerated at all.

EARLY TIMES

People with various disabilities have been born into societies around the globe and throughout history. In some places, such as ancient Greece, people who had seizures and mental disorders were thought to have connections with the gods. But most people with both mental and physical challenges were considered to be imperfect and lesser human beings. The ancient philosopher Aristotle even believed that children born with physical defects shouldn't be allowed to live.

In general, people with disabilities had hard lives. Their families may not have supported them. Society in general rejected them, whether they were blind, born with malformed limbs, or had a mental disorder. They were shunned by most members of society, were not given any help, and often led lives of poverty.

Eventually, things began to change. In the 1700s and 1800s, some people realized that society shouldn't just give up on people with disabilities. Schools were built around Europe that catered to different challenges. The first school for the deaf was established in Germany in 1755. The first American school for the deaf was founded in Hartford, Connecticut, in 1817.

INSTITUTIONALIZATION

Much of the time, however, people still didn't know what to do with those who had mental or physical challenges. At the time, no one thought that they could live independent

The American School for the Deaf in West Hartford, Connecticut

and fulfilling lives. Sometimes families took care of these individuals, but many people with disabilities were put into institutions. They were confined there, away from the rest of the world, for their entire lives.

The first American **residential institution** for people with mental challenges was built in 1848, in Boston. Generally, people with mental disabilities were not considered able to function in society at large. Families had once kept them hidden away, and now they were usually put in institutions, under medical care. Some institutions were **legitimate** medical operations, trying to help people, but others were no better than jails.

One person who did a lot of good for people with disabilities during this time was Dorothea Dix. She spent many years fighting for the rights of people with mental disabilities, and she urged American states to set up better care for them.

Dorothea Dix

She had dozens of mental hospitals set up, providing more appropriate care for people with mental disabilities.

By the middle of the twentieth century, most people, however, knew that institutions had failed. There were too many people living in the facilities. They weren't "curing" people or helping them learn to live in the outside world. And stories of abuse and neglect horrified people. Many institutions closed their doors. The people who were discharged sometimes ended up homeless or in jail. No one had prepared them for taking care of themselves.

THE FREAK SHOW

Back in the nineteenth and early twentieth centuries, some people with disabilities were put on display, not hidden away in institutions. Circuses and freak shows attracted huge audiences, all to see people who looked different. P.T. Barnum and other imitators set up traveling shows that featured mostly people with physical disabilities. Included among the "freaks" were people without arms or legs, exceptionally hairy individuals, and people who were unusually short or tall. Crowds flocked to see these individuals; their differences fascinated people—but they also got in the way of people perceiving them as human.

Eugenics

One of the saddest times in the history of disability was the rise of the eugenics movement. In the United States and in Europe, people started thinking that they could make human populations "better." They thought that a group of people could be improved by controlling who had children with whom. People who were stronger and smarter were considered more desirable than other people.

This led to a lot of scary things. The Eugenics Record Office (ERO) was established in the United States in 1910. One committee of the ERO decided that 10 percent of the American population was defective, and shouldn't be allowed to reproduce. Included in this number were people with disabilities. Tens of thousands of disabled people were **sterilized**.

Nazi Germany

One place that eugenic theories took hold was in Nazi Germany. As Adolf Hitler rose to power, he spread his ideas of racial superiority. According to Hitler, Aryans (white, blond-haired, blue-eyed Europeans) were the best race. Everyone else, including Jews, Gypsies, and people with disabilities, were inferior. Even worse, according to Hitler, they should be exterminated.

Under Hitler, thousands of people with disabilities were sterilized. There were laws that prevented them from getting married. Children with disabilities were killed.

People with disabilities suffered during the Holocaust along with Jews, Gypsies, and homosexuals. People that the Nazis thought were undesirable were sent to concentration camps to work, and eventually to die. Hitler's official program aimed at getting rid of disabled people was called T4. The program killed 275,000 people.

TODAY

Today, things are starting to look a little different for people with mental and physical challenges. Starting in the mid-1900s, Americans started realizing that disabilities did not mean that a person had to be institutionalized or considered a victim. Some people started speaking out for more rights for those with disabilities.

In 1968, the first Special Olympics was held in Chicago. Public spaces became handicapped accessible and laws were passed protecting people's rights. President Ronald Reagan even designated 1983 to 1992 as the National Decade of Disabled Persons.

Although things are looking up for people with disabilities, prejudice has not gone away. Kids are ridiculed in school for being different, people are made fun of or pointed at for their appearance or behavior, and they are still subject to many stereotypes surrounding disabilities.

Special Olympics

The Special Olympics is a worldwide event for athletes with disabilities. Every other year, the Special Olympics are held in a different city, alternating between the summer and winter games. The Special Olympics has local chapters that host a variety of sporting competitions and health events. It inspires people with disabilities to follow their dreams, no matter where they are.

A thousand people participated in the very first Special Olympics in 1968. At the most recent games in 2011 in Athens, Greece, 7,000 athletes participated, from 170 different countries.

The Special Olympics gives people with disabilities the opportunity to compete with each other athletically.

Famous Disabled People

- **Jim Abbott:** Abbott was a professional baseball player born without a right hand. It didn't stop him from playing with major teams and throwing a famous no-hitter with the Yankees in 1993.

- **Beethoven:** This famous composer became deaf as an adult. He wrote many of his most well-known pieces after he lost his hearing.

- **Stephen Hawking:** Diagnosed with Lou Gehrig's Disease (ALS), Hawking is an influential physicist and mathematician who is a quadriplegic and uses a wheelchair.

- **Helen Keller:** Keller was blind, deaf, and mute, but used her talents to help other people with disabilities lead better lives.

- **Christopher Reeve:** As an actor, Reeve played Superman. He was in a horse-riding accident that caused him to become a quadriplegic, which inspired him to educate others about his condition.

- **Franklin D. Roosevelt:** The thirty-second President is the only person to have served more than two terms as the leader of the United States, through the Great Depression and the first years of World War II. Roosevelt also had polio and spent most of his time in a wheelchair.

- **Harriet Tubman:** Tubman was one of the most active people helping slaves escape from the South before the Civil War. When she was young, Tubman was struck on the head by an overseer, and had periodic seizures the rest of her life.
- **Stevie Wonder:** This famous singer was born blind. He is one of the most successful musicians of all time, winning Grammy Awards and earning fans everywhere.

There are even more alarming instances of prejudice crossing the line into violence. For example, in February of 2011, a mentally challenged woman was taken hostage and tortured for days before being killed. Only some states have **hate crime** legislation targeted at disabled people; many do not. Yet people with disabilities are at greater risk for being victims of violent crime and sexual assaults.

While there is still a long way to go, a lot of people are standing up for their rights, including those with disabilities themselves.

Real-Life Stories

R achel H. shared her story in Tourette Perspectives, which was republished on www.listentoourstories. com. Rachel has **Tourette syndrome**, which has had a big impact on her life.

I was eight when I was diagnosed with Tourette syndrome. At that age I did not want to deal with a disorder. At the time, my life was pretty smooth. I owned as many Barbies as my friends, and though void of the Barbie motor home, I did have a Mattel swing set. I was just like my friends,

Dealing with a disability can make a child feel left out. Other children who make fun of differences can make her feel still worse.

and I, the **idealist**, believed it could stay that way. But soon my Tourette became more pronounced and I had to deal with the questions we all want to avoid: "Why do you wrinkle your nose? Why do you make clucking noises?" In an effort to avoid these questions, I avoided people. I figured if no one noticed me, no one would notice my Tourette. Yet this withdrawn behavior made me even more different.

By seventh grade I was absolutely miserable. I had no friends. In a school of conformity, I could not conform, and for the first time, having a learning disability began to affect my grades and performance. I was filled with frustration when I was penalized for "careless errors." But I still would not accept extra help, for accepting extra help would be accepting that I was different. And it was this resistance to believing that I truly was not like my peers that caused my improvement to come to a standstill. It was hard to come to terms with and accept my Tourette, but once I did, I completed the first step to subduing my Tourette. . . .

I finally understood and accepted the fact that I was different and I could not change that. I was born different, but I was not born wrong. There is nothing unnatural about having Tourette syndrome. So I blink my eyes twice as fast as everyone else. Where does it say that is wrong? It is a different way of behaving but not a wrong one. Take the example of left-handed people. Lefties are also in the minority, as are we. Lefties write differently, as we act differently. There are strikes against left-handers that the right-hander does not have. I know, as I too have struggled to keep my papers balanced on a right-handed desk and fight against right-handed appliances everywhere. Yet though it may be difficult to be a left-hander, we do not consider a left-handed trait negative, and we should not consider Tourette to be a negative trait. As I am not ashamed to be one of the few chosen to write with the opposite hand, I am also not ashamed to be one of the chosen to have developed and tamed Tourette.

Rachel struggled in school and in social situations for a long time. But her story shows that disabilities are not just challenges; they can also be ways of growing and of becoming stronger as a person.

Naeem Ahmed also shared his story on the same website. He grew up with cerebral palsy, moving from Bangladesh to the United States when he was six.

I think almost everyone that I've met, if they really get to know me, they stick to me like magnets! Or I help them out, they help me out. Y'know? Like, after I meet someone, they open the floodgates, should we say. So I think making friends is really easy for me. But there's always been like one or two people that didn't really wanta know me. Because some kids or teenagers or whatever are really tentative about, y'know, talking to people who have a little bit of a disability or look weird to them or are not smart as they are. In those situations I just talk to them, do different things, and, hopefully, the friendship will develop. Or if not friends, he or she gets to know a little bit more about me so he won't feel like I'm a stranger to him or he's a stranger to me. . . .

Like sometimes, when some kids really don't wanta be that open, if it's a really nice person and they don't wanta get to know me, that can get really frustrating for me! But I just think it over or talk to my parents about it and usually, after a while, I keep pushing on the button so much that they have to open the doors. That can really be a thrill— making friends that really don't wanta be your friends at first. It's like climbing K2 or any other big mountain you might find.

I hafta really push myself a lot harder than any able-bodied person would, just to get myself up and, like, play a sport or do a activity or something. People have always told me that most of the time I'm really persistent in whatever I'm doing. I think in most cases, if you're persistent, you'll eventually get there. It might take you much longer than it would take an able-bodied person, but you can get there eventually. I mean, just knowing that really helps me on my day-to-day life and experiences. . . .

Living with a disability, sometimes it gets hard because some buildings don't have wheelchair or walker accessibility or whatever. And I think that really needs to change. If restaurants or all buildings had more of that, more people with disabilities would come out to them and really go in. I think people high up need to try to be more aware of

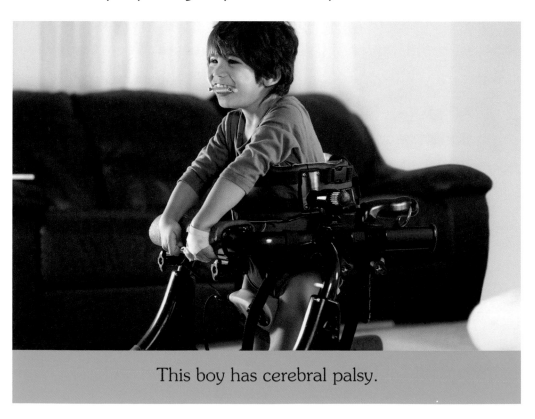

This boy has cerebral palsy.

Mental and Physical Challenges

people with disabilities. I know they're trying to be—I'm not criticizing anybody or anything—but maybe try to be, like, a little more aware. And people with disability always, I think, have to try to let their voices be heard a bit more. Y'know, my parents always tell me when I don't tell them something, "Tell us what the problem is or what's going on, or how we gonna help?"

On a last note: I think in their daily lives, people with disabilities have to have hope. Because sometimes we all have bad days, but if we really have hope and couple of people that we can really depend on, we'll eventually get through it and we'll be able to use our full potential

Naeem also faced a lot of challenges because of his disability, like making friends, social acceptance, and moving around in public spaces. But he too, like Rachel, learned to live with those challenges and eventually wasn't afraid to speak out. His self-confidence and belief in himself shine through his words!

Brittany is another teenager who faces a different kind of disability. She says, "Before June of 2005 sports were what my life was about. I played soccer for school, a travel team, and was on both the indoor and outdoor track teams for my high school. I even made varsity track as an eighth-grader. I have always been the girl that none of the boys wanted to race in gym class for the simple reason that no boy wanted to 'lose to a girl.'"

Then in June 2005, everything changed for Brittany. "I first noticed there was something wrong after running in a track meet. My knee didn't feel right. I went to see the athletic trainer and began physical therapy because we thought it was just a pulled muscle. It never crossed my mind that it could be cancer. When the doctors told me that I had osteosarcoma, a bone cancer, my world fell apart."

It turned out that Brittany had a tumor in her leg, just above her knee. "Everything was a blur," she remembers, "and I never fully accepted or understood how much it was going to change my life. I was told I would need chemotherapy, surgery, then even more chemotherapy, and that I would have to start right away. I wasn't even allowed to finish the school year. . . . I had limb-salvage surgery on August 30, 2005, the extent of which is still overwhelming to me. It's the hardest thing I had to deal with. I had a total knee replacement, and rods replaced part of my upper and lower leg. The recovery was hard; there are no words to fully describe the extreme pain. But the physical pain is easy compared to the emotional pain that comes with the new rules I now have to live by for the rest of my life: no running or impact on my leg! For me this means my life will never be the same. No more track and no more soccer.

"I was blindsided by this and took it harder than finding out that I had cancer. Right up to the moment before surgery, I prayed it was all a big mistake and I wouldn't need the surgery. I even threatened my parents with running away just to keep my knee so I could play soccer.

"I have to fight back the tears every time I visit the track or soccer field. Sometimes it's really hard and I have to turn back before I even get there. My coaches and teammates have all been very supportive. At first I tried to remain an active member of all my teams, but it was too hard to deal with, so I found a new way to remain active in sports; I am helping to coach a girl's travel soccer team for the local Soccer Association and I love every minute of it. Even though I cannot play, my love for soccer and track will never go away.

"The good news is that after surgery the biopsy showed that the chemotherapy worked. One hundred percent of the cancer cells had been killed! . . . Every day, I thank God that I have my life back and get to do normal teenage stuff. . . . I

Cancer survivors sometimes face prejudice.

Mental and Physical Challenges

have no idea what the future holds, but there is one thing I know for sure: I will make the best of every situation and live life to the fullest. I kicked cancer. I can do anything!"

Like Rachel and Naeem, it's evident how much Brittany has grown as a person because of the disability she faces. But she has also faced prejudice from those around her. Another cancer survivor Brittany's age points out that "people hear the word cancer and they feel sorry for you and just assume that you're going to die. People are also afraid of getting close to you—I think that even though they know it isn't contagious, there are still some superstitious feelings out there that you might catch it."

People like Rachel, Naeem, and Brittany do a lot to fight prejudice and fear against people with disabilities. By speaking up and helping people understand what they experience, they are doing their part to overcome prejudice. And each of us can do our part to help them in this fight!

Fighting Prejudice

At the very beginning of the United States, when the thirteen original colonies first declared their independence from England on July 4, 1776, they stated that all "are created equal, that they are endowed by their Creator with certain **unalienable** rights, that among them are Life, Liberty, and the pursuit of happiness."

America's history is the story of how it has struggled to live up to these ideals. Civil rights are those rights guaranteed to all U.S. citizens by the U.S. **Constitution**, the Bill of Rights, and additional constitutional **amendments**. They include personal rights (freedom of speech, freedom to peaceably assemble, freedom to bear arms, freedom of the press, freedom from unreasonable search and seizure, and freedom of religion) and legal rights (the right to not incriminate yourself, the right to have a speedy trial by jury, and protection from cruel and unusual punishment). Later amendments added more civil rights: The thirteenth amendment eliminated slavery in the United States; the fifteenth and nineteenth amendments gave the right to vote to minorities and women; and the twenty-sixth amendment gave the right to vote to all people over eighteen years of age. These laws provide basics rights for all U.S. citizens.

But not everyone in the United States could actually take advantage of these rights. Prejudice and **discrimination** often got in the way. In 1866, however, the Civil Rights Act won a small victory in the battle against prejudice, stating that "all persons shall have the same rights . . . to make and enforce contracts, to sue, be parties, give evidence, and to the full and equal benefit of all laws."

Meanwhile, Canada was fighting its own battles against this form of prejudice. The International Year of Disabled Persons 1981 triggered a new awareness of this issue, and the following year, the inclusion of physical and mental disability under Section 15 of the Canadian Charter of Rights and Freedoms marked the first time in history that any national Constitution referred specifically to persons with disabilities. This became a model for the entire world to imitate, because it framed disability as a citizenship and human rights issue. In 1987, a parliamentary committee on Human Rights and the Status of Disabled Persons was made a permanent body that consults with people with disabilities and makes recommendations to Parliament.

President Lyndon B. Johnson signs the 1964 Civil Rights Act as Martin Luther King, Jr., and others, look on.

ADA Definitions

WHO IS AN "INDIVIDUAL WITH A DISABILITY?"

Section 504 of the Rehabilitation Act of 1973 and the ADA define an "individual with a disability" three ways: (a) a person who has a physical or mental impairment that substantially limits one or more major life activities, (b) a person who has a history or record of such an impairment, or (c) a person who is perceived by others as having such an impairments. Unlike the IDEA, the ADA does not identify or list all specific disabilities and conditions it covers.

WHAT DOES "SUBSTANTIALLY LIMITS" MEAN?

Section 504 of the Rehabilitation Act of 1973 defines "substantially limits" as being unable to perform a major life activity, or significantly restricted as to the condition, manner, or duration under which a major life activity can be performed, in comparison to the average person or to most people. The ADA uses the same definition.

WHAT IS A "MAJOR LIFE ACTIVITY?"

According to Section 504 of the Rehabilitation Act of 1973, a major life activity is defined as caring for oneself, performing manual tasks, walking, seeing, hearing, speaking, breathing, learning, reading, writing, performing math calculations, and working. The ADA also uses this definition.

In 1990, in the United States, the Americans with Disabilities Act (ADA) was passed. This was a huge step in the right direction. First, the act defined what disability is: "a physical or mental impairment that substantially limits a major life activity." The act also granted many civil rights to people with disabilities. Until the act became law, those with disabilities had often faced great barriers to fulfilling their civil rights. Take voting in a local election, for example: How could a woman in a wheelchair exercise her right to vote if her wheelchair couldn't fit through the polling place door? How could a blind man vote if the ballot wasn't available in Braille? The act also prevented discrimination in employment, public transportation, government services, and **telecommunications** services, among other things.

Also, in 1990, the U.S. government passed the Individuals with Disabilities Education Act (IDEA). This act ensured that all children with disabilities would get an education that is appropriate for them, and that would prepare them for a life outside of school.

Before these laws were passed, prejudice against disabilities often took these forms:

- Students with physical, psychological, or learning challenges went to school, but they were segregated from the "normal" kids.
- Restaurants who welcomed most customers turned blind people away because they used Seeing Eye Dogs ("No dogs allowed").
- Bus drivers refused to pick up those who used wheelchairs because the buses' narrow doors and steps made it too bothersome to help them.
- Employers wouldn't hire people with epilepsy because they didn't want an employee having a seizure on the job.

Making sure that laws protect all people's rights is an important step in the fight against prejudice—ultimately, prejudice is something that lives inside people. No law can change the way a person thinks about others. That's something we have to do. We do it by changing the way we talk and act. We do it by changing the way we think.

CELEBRATING DIVERSITY

One of the first things that has to change is the way we think about differences. Instead of being frightened of the ways people are different from ourselves, we need to start feeling curious and interested. We need to be willing to learn from people who are different. We need to enjoy the differences!

Most people enjoy diversity when it comes to the world around them. They like different kinds of food. They read different kinds of books. They enjoy different kinds of music and television shows. The world would be pretty boring if everything was exactly the same!

People are also diverse, in the same way as the rest of the world is. Although all of us feel the same basic emotions—sadness and happiness, anger and laughter, loneliness and pride, jealousy and compassion, to name just a few—and most of us look a lot alike (we are all human after all!), we also are different in many ways. Our hair, eyes, and skin come

Fighting Prejudice 53

in different colors. Our brains can do different things. Our noses are big or little or something in between. Our bodies are different sizes and shapes and have different abilities. And when you get down to the details—to our fingerprints and the DNA inside our cells—we're absolutely unique, despite all the things we have in common with other human beings. Each of us looks at the world a little differently. We believe different things. And we offer different things as well.

The world is a richer place because of all this human diversity. You can learn from and enjoy your friends because, although they're like you in some ways, they're also different from you in other ways. Those differences make them interesting! And in a similar way, we can learn from human beings' different abilities, different languages, different ways of thinking about God, and different lifestyles.

Prejudice, however, focuses on the differences in a negative way. It doesn't value all that differences have to offer us. Instead, it divides people into in-groups and out-groups. It breaks the Golden Rule.

Do you recognize prejudice when you hear it? Sometimes it's hard. We get so used to certain ways of thinking that we

become blind to what's really going on. But anytime you hear people being lumped together, chances are prejudice is going on. Statements like these are all signs of prejudice:

Poor kids smell bad.
Girls run funny.
Old people are boring.
Special ed kids are weird.
Jocks are jerks.

Rather than building bridges between people, prejudice puts up walls. It makes it hard to talk to others or understand them. And those walls can lead to hatred, violence, and even wars.

A first step to ending prejudice is speaking up against it whenever you hear it. Point it out when you hear your friends or family being prejudiced. They may not even realize that's what they're being.

But even more important, you need to spot prejudice when it's inside you. That's not always easy, of course. Here are some ways experts suggest you can fight prejudice when you find it inside yourself:

1. Learn more about groups of people who are different from you. Read books about their history; read fiction that allows you to walk in their shoes in your imagination; watch movies that portray them accurately.

2. Get to know people who are different from you. Practice being a good listener, focusing on what they have to say rather than on your own opinions and experiences. Ask about others' backgrounds and family stories.

3. Practice compassion. Imagine what it would feel like to be someone who is different from you. Your imagination is a powerful tool you can use to make the world better!

4. Believe in yourself. Surprisingly, a lot of the time, psychologists say, prejudice is caused by having a bad self-concept. If you don't like who you are and you don't believe in your own abilities, you're more likely to be scared and threatened by others. People who are comfortable with themselves are also more comfortable with people who are different from themselves.

Making public buildings accessible to people in wheelchairs is actually a way to protect their civil rights.

Five Ways to Use Words to Fight Prejudice Against People Facing Challenges

1. Don't say: "John *is an epileptic*." (This focuses on the disease, not the person)

   DO say: "John *has epilepsy*" or "John is a person *who has epilepsy*" instead.

2. Don't say: "Suzie struggles with cerebral palsy." (This makes her condition negative.)

   DO say: "Suzie is *affected* by cerebral palsy."

3. Don't say: "Dwaine *is confined* to a wheelchair" or "Dwaine is wheelchair bound." (This assumes wheelchairs restrict those who use them when, in fact, wheelchairs provide great freedom to the mobility challenged.)

   DO say: "Dwaine *uses* a wheelchair," or "Dwaine *is a wheelchair user*."

4. Don't say: "Maria is *afflicted* by" or "*suffers* from depression." (This focuses on the negative and makes Maria a victim.)

DO say: "Maria was *diagnosed with* depression" or "Maria *has a depressive disorder*."

5. Don't describe those with challenges as "crippled" or "handicapped." (This focuses on inability and limitation)

DO describe them as people "with challenges" or as "differently-abled."

What does it all come down to in the end? Perhaps the war against prejudice can best be summed up with just two words— communication and respect.

FIND OUT MORE

In Books

Burch, Susan. *Encyclopedia of American History.* New York: Facts on File, Inc, 2009.

Leicester, Mal. *Special Stories for Disability Awareness.* London, UK: Jessica Kingsley Publishers, 2007.

Pelka, Fred. *What We Have Done.* Amherst, Mass.: University of Massachusetts Press, 2012.

On the Internet

AMERICAN ASSOCIATION OF PEOPLE WITH DISABILITIES
www.aapd.com

DISABILITY.GOV
www.disability.gov

MUSEUM OF DISABILITY
www.museumofdisability.org

UNITED NATIONS
www.un.org/disabilities/index.asp

GLOSSARY

amendments: Changes to the U.S. Constitution.

autism: A disorder in which a person is unable to communicate in a normal, social way.

bipolar disorder: A condition that involves extreme mood swings between very good and very bad periods.

constitution: The document that founds and guides a government.

discrimination: Unjust treatment of someone because of their race, ethnicity, gender, or other characteristic.

effeminate: Overly feminine; usually used as an insult.

hate crime: A crime committed against someone because of their race, ethnicity, gender, or other prejudice.

idealist: A person who believes that something can be perfect.

legitimate: Lawful and right.

obsessive compulsive disorder (OCD): An anxiety disorder characterized by unreasonable and repetitive actions.

oversimplification: Making something complicated too simple.

quadriplegia: Unable to move all four limbs.

residential institution: A live-in hospital.

schizophrenia: A mental disorder that is characterized by being unable to tell the difference between reality and thoughts.

sociologists: People who study that way that humans behave.

sterilized: To make someone unable to have children.

stigmatize: To make something be considered as shameful.

telecommunications: Communications over a long distance, such as on the phone or over email.

Tourette syndrome: A disorder that involves repetitive and uncontrollable movements or sounds.

unalienable: Unable to be taken away or separated from.

vulnerability: The state of being open to danger of some sort.

INDEX

BIBLIOGRAPHY

ACCESS! "The Top Ten Stereotypes for People with Disabilities." www.accessuvic.ca/student-accessibility-issues8.html.

Burch, Susan. *Encyclopedia of American History.* New York: Facts on File, Inc, 2009.

eNotes. "People with Disabilities." 2012. www.enotes.com/disabilities-people-with-reference/disabilities-people-with.

Fleisher, D. and Zames, F. *The Disability Rights Movement: From Charity to Confrontation.* Philadelphia, Pa.: Temple University Press, 2001.

Listen to Our Stories. 2008. www.listentoourstories.com/index.htm.

The Minnesota Governor's Council on Developmental Disabilities. "Parallels in Time: A History of Developmental Disability." www.mnddc.org/parallels/index.html.

Museum of DisAbility. 2011. www.museumofdisability.org/home.asp.

Soulful Encounters. "Famous Disabled People." www.soulfulencounters.com/AboutUs/FamousDisabledPeople/tabid/85/Default.aspx.

United Nations. "Combating Discrimination against Persons with Disabilities." UN Office of the High Commissioner for Human Rights. www.ohchr.org/EN/ABOUTUS/Pages/DiscriminationAgainst-PersonsWithDisabilities.aspx.

United States Holocaust Memorial Museum. "People with Disabilities." www.ushmm.org/research/library/bibliography/?lang=en&content=people_with_disabilities.

Picture Credits

About the Author

Ellyn Sanna is the author of hundreds of books for children, young adults, and adults. She has also worked for many years as an editor and small-business owner.